World Faiths Today Series
Exploring Buddhism

Who are your friends? Do you k... them? Do they know everything ...

Well, this is a story about friends who d... about one another. But they are starting ... ...gs their friends do and why they do them. Read t... story and you might learn something new too!

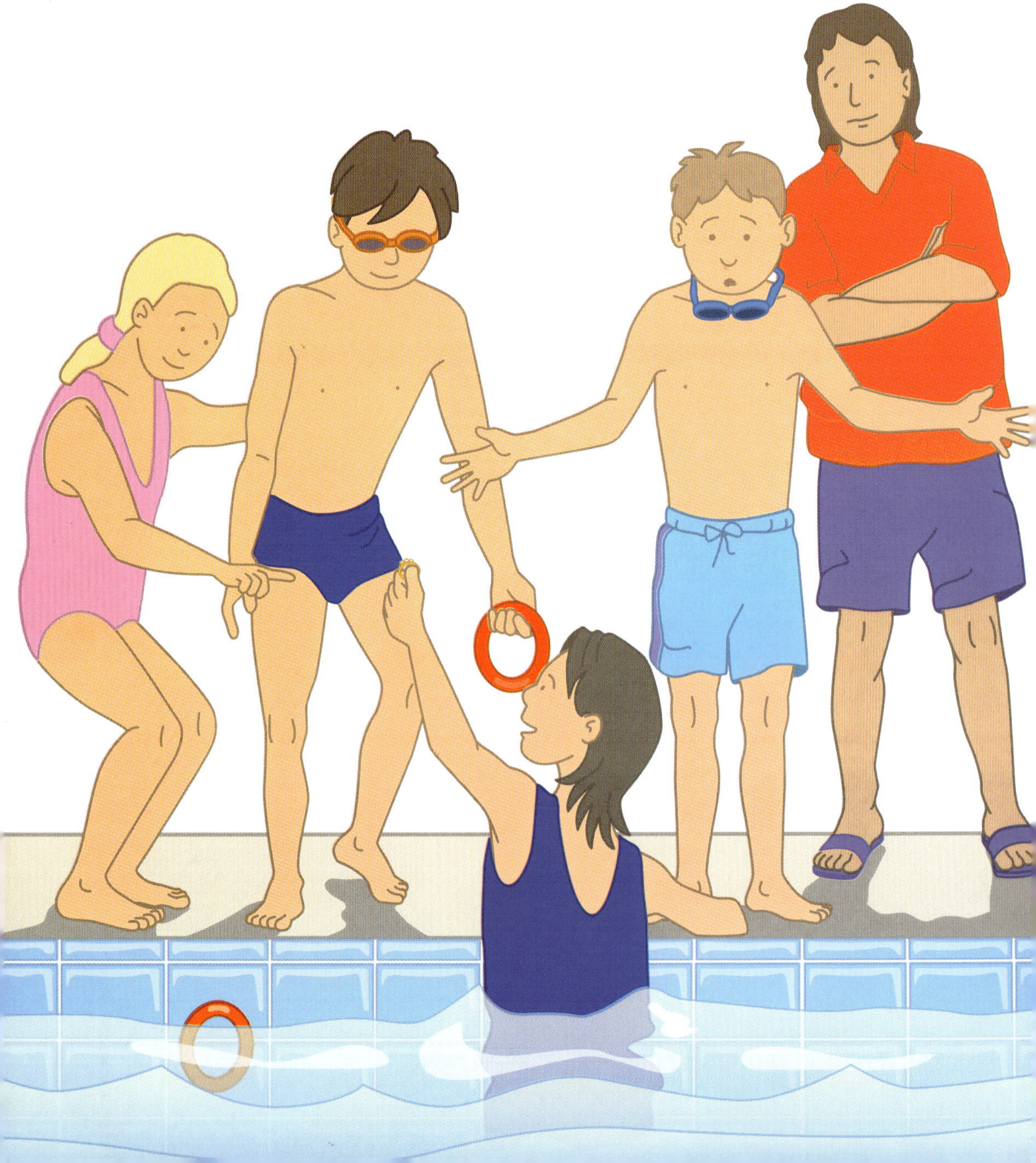

1 Visiting a Buddhist centre

'Get a move on, Rees!' said Sara impatiently. Rees waved a pair of swimming trunks in the air.

'I have found them!' he cried, ramming them untidily into a bag with his goggles and towel. Their friends, James and Hana, were waiting for them outside. James and Hana lived next door. Rees and Sara often spent time with them at weekends. James and Hana were Buddhists.

At the swimming pool, the children threw weighted rings into the water. They had a competition to see who could collect the most in one go.

Sara did a shallow dive and headed towards the rings. Something distracted her and she fumbled around the bottom of the pool. Rees, James, and Hana exchanged puzzled looks. What was she doing?

Sara surfaced and spluttered and gasped for breath. Her left hand was clasped into a fist.

'Guess what I have found,' she grinned.

Opening her hand slowly and carefully, she whispered, 'A gold ring.'

'It must be very precious,' said Hana. 'The ring has three diamonds and it looks old. Perhaps it is a family heirloom.'

The children gave the ring to the lifeguard so that it could be given back to its owner.

'Buddhism is like that ring,' said James. 'It has three precious jewels too. Come and see them in our Buddhist Centre.'

At the Buddhist Centre, Rees and Sara removed their shoes and stepped into the shrine room. In front of them was an enormous shrine. On the shrine sat a large golden statue. The statue's eyes were half-closed and a faint smile touched the corners of the statue's mouth. There were many other smaller statues on the shrine too.

'Our first Jewel is Buddha,' said Hana. 'The big statue is Buddha Shakyamuni. He lived in India around 560 BCE. There are lots of other Buddhas as well. A Buddha is someone who is truly happy. Most Buddhas teach others how to be truly happy as well.'

Rees and Sara saw some Buddhists bow in front of the shrine and make offerings of food, light, water, and flowers. They chanted in English from books placed on low tables. A man dressed in a maroon coloured robe sat in front of the others. 'He is our teacher,' said James.

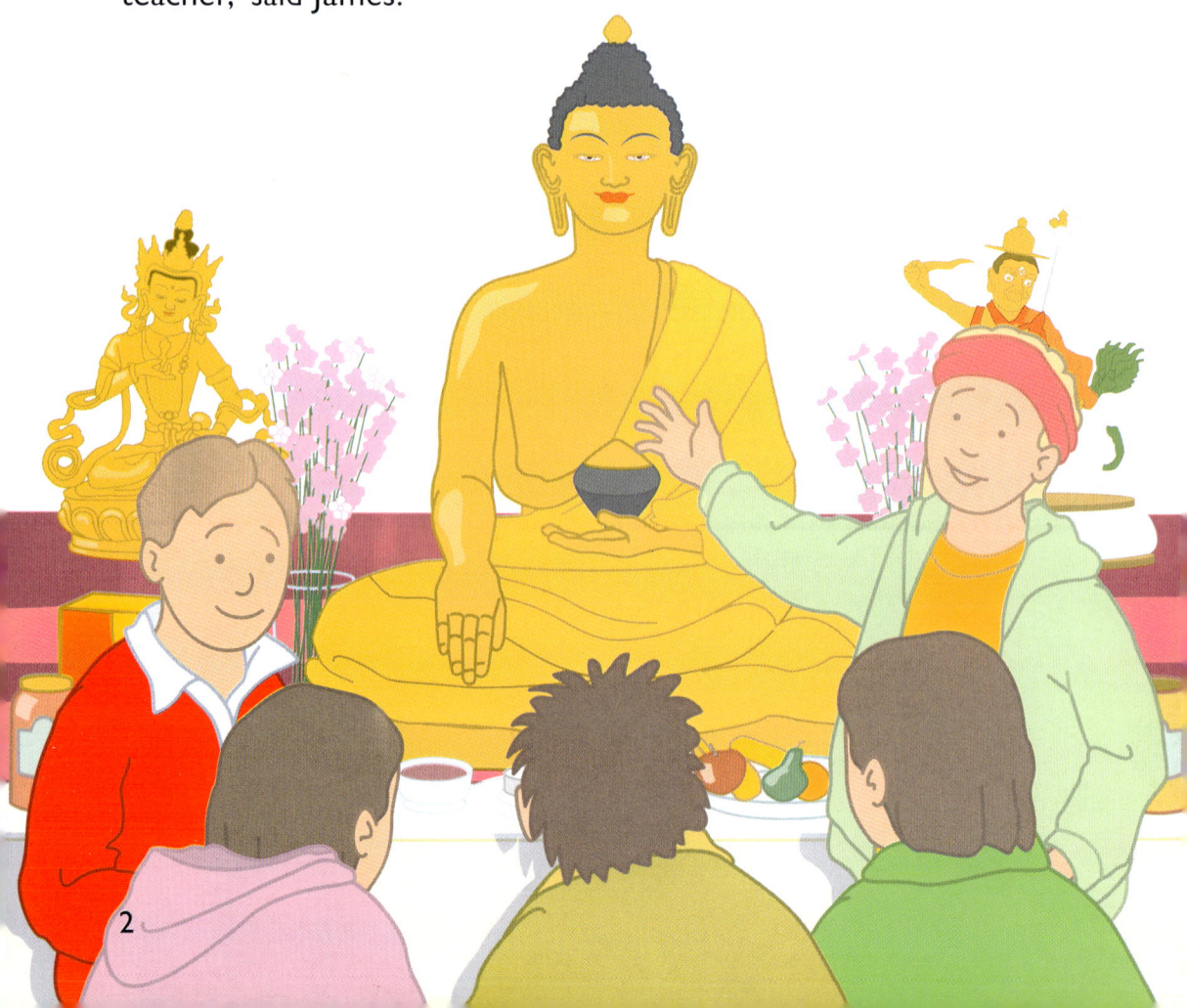

James pointed to a pile of books wrapped up in material on the shrine.

'Our second Jewel is Dharma. Dharma is the teachings which have been passed down to us. The teachings help to guide us along the Buddhist path to true happiness. They show us what we should believe and how we should act.'

'Our third Jewel is Sangha,' said Hana, pointing towards the people in front of the shrine. 'Sangha is our Buddhist family or community. Buddhists believe that living together as a community is very important. There is a story which explains why.'

Hana told them the story about the king's elephant.

A king had a favourite elephant. The elephant was kind and gentle and the king was very fond of it. One day the king became worried about his elephant. It had started to behave out of character. It had become bad tempered and irritable and nobody could understand why. One of the king's advisors had an idea. Someone would secretly stay in the elephant's quarters overnight and watch the elephant. Perhaps they would discover why the elephant was behaving so oddly.

The secret watcher indeed discovered something. Thieves were using the elephant's sleeping quarters as a meeting place to plan their next raid. Night after night, the elephant listened to quarrelsome voices filled with greed and hatred. Bad company was making the elephant feel bad tempered and irritable. The thieves were arrested and the elephant was surrounded by love and kindness. Over time, the elephant became kind and gentle once more.

James explained, 'Buddhists believe that it is easier to be with people who want the same things as you do. Everyone can then help one another to follow the Buddhist path.'

At the Buddhist Centre Rees and Sara had learnt that James and Hana believe in Three Jewels. These Jewels are called Buddha, Dharma, and Sangha. Together, the Three Jewels help them to follow the Buddhist path leading to real happiness.

6

2 A children's festival

Rees and Sara ran across the field, weaving their way around caravans, camper vans, and tents. It was the start of a warm, sunny day in early May.

'James and Hana are over there,' said Sara, heading towards two children who were playing beside one of the caravans. James and Hana were attending a weekend Buddhist children's festival with their family. Families and their friends from different parts of the country were there to learn more about Buddhism and to have fun at the same time.

There were lots of exciting things to do. There were workshops for art, drama, and meditation. There was even a workshop which taught families how to follow the Buddhist path in their daily lives. But perhaps the best part of all was meeting old friends and making new ones.

James and Hana were pleased to see Rees and Sara.

'You have arrived in time to rehearse the play,' said Hana. 'The play is about the life of Buddha Shakyamuni. Buddha Shakyamuni lived on earth over 2,500 years ago as a man called Siddhartha Gautama. The play is about his life and teachings.'

Siddhartha Gautama was born into a wealthy and powerful family in northern India. A wise man predicted that the child would grow up to be either a powerful world ruler or a great religious teacher. Siddhartha's father wanted him to grow up to be a powerful world ruler so he surrounded his son with beautiful things. He also made sure Siddhartha was trained in all the skills necessary for a strong ruler.

One day Siddhartha travelled outside the comfort of his beautiful home with one of his servants. He saw Four Sights that were to change his life forever. The First Sight was a sick person. The Second Sight was an old person. The Third Sight was a dead person. Siddhartha realised that everyone becomes sick, grows old, and dies. Nothing lasts forever. This thought made him sad.

Finally, Siddhartha saw the Fourth Sight. A holy man walked past him. The holy man's face looked peaceful and happy.

'He must have found a cure for suffering!' Siddhartha thought.

Siddhartha left his beautiful home and joined a group of holy men. He starved and punished his body, hoping to find the cure for suffering. But he did not.

Eventually Siddhartha left the holy men and sat under a tree and meditated. He vowed to stay there until he found a cure for suffering. By the end of the night, he succeeded! He finally understood why people suffer and how to cure them. At this moment, he became Buddha – one who is fully awake and sees things for what they really are.

Buddha Shakyamuni spent the rest of his earthly life teaching others what he had learnt.

Rees and Sara enjoyed rehearsing the play. Their heads were filled with questions they wanted to ask about the story.

'What exactly did Siddhartha do under the tree?' asked Rees. 'What is meditation? It must be something very important if it helped Siddhartha discover a cure for suffering.'

'There is a meditation workshop we can go to,' answered Hana. 'Maybe you will find the answer to your question there.'

In the meditation workshop Rees and Sara were taught how to sit and breathe properly. This made them feel calm and peaceful. It also helped them to concentrate.

'People's minds are busy things,' said James. 'People's minds are so busy that it is difficult to think about important things properly. That is why Siddhartha meditated under the tree. Meditating helped his mind to feel calm and peaceful. Meditating also helped him to think very hard about suffering and how to cure it.'

Rees and Sara felt tired and happy after their day at the Buddhist children's festival. They had learnt that the festival was a time for Buddhist families from around the country to get together and discover more about Buddhism. They also had learnt that Buddhists believe that they know why people are unhappy and suffer. Buddhists also believe that they know how to stop this suffering so people can be truly happy.

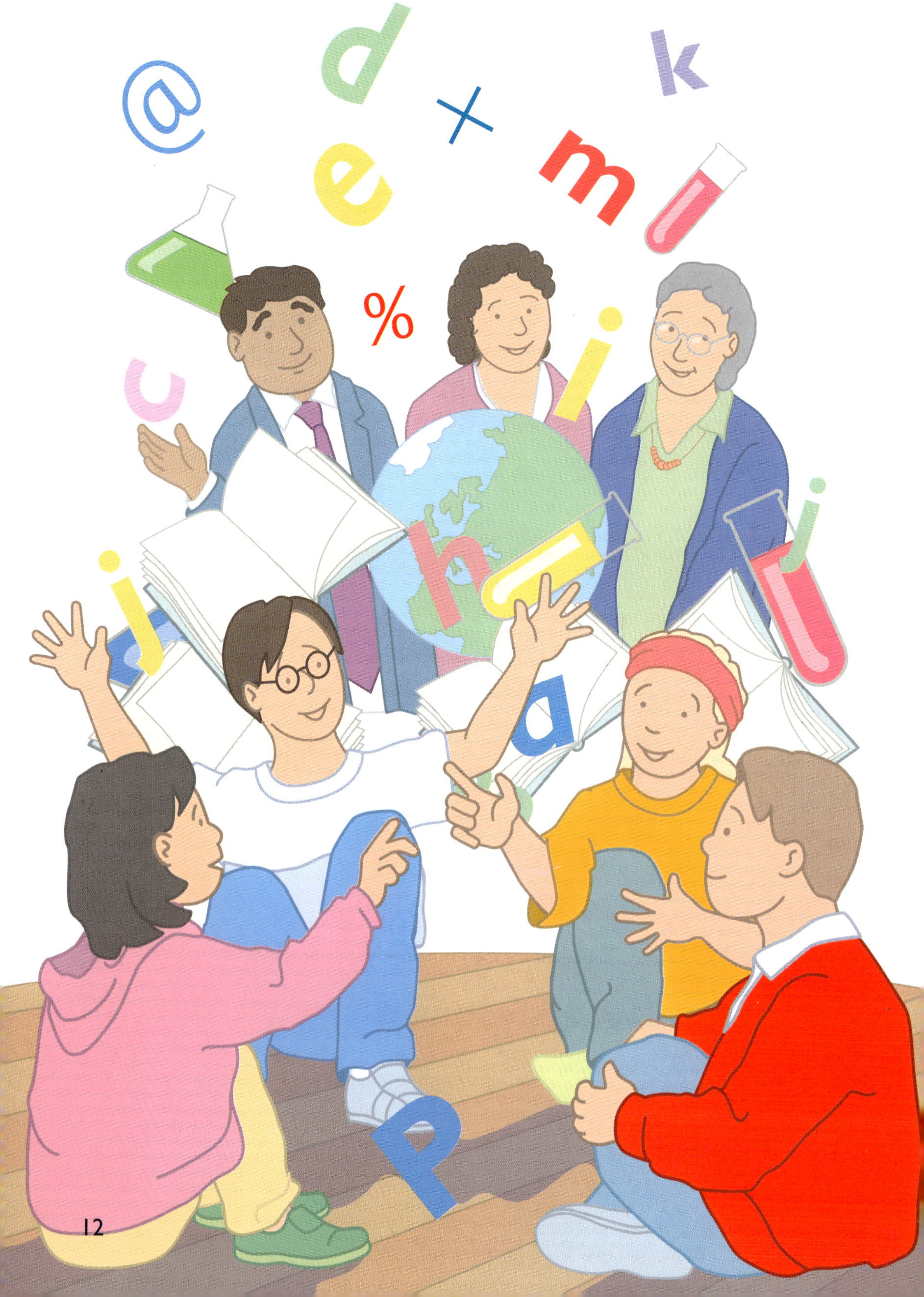

3 Teachers

Rees and Sara sat on the floor in James' bedroom. They were having an argument with their friends, James and Hana, about who was the best teacher in their school.

'What about Mr Roberts?' suggested Rees. 'He makes me laugh and his lessons are fun. I learn a lot when I am enjoying myself.'

'Mrs Jones is a good teacher,' said Sara. 'She is kind and patient when I do not understand things. She explains things again and again until I understand.'

'Mrs Edwards is good teacher too,' said James. 'She is strict but fair. When I am lazy or misbehave, I get into trouble. But when I do my best and follow the rules, I get house points.'

Hana frowned and thought hard. 'Teachers are very different from one another,' she said. 'Some are fun, some are kind and patient, and some are strict but fair. I think a good teacher is anyone who knows how to help people learn things. You can help people learn things in many different ways.'

The children thought about what they were taught at school – maths, language, science, and other subjects. All of these would help them to understand the world when they grew up.

'We have teachers in Buddhism as well,' said James. 'They teach us important things about life and about the world too. An important part of the teachings is the Four Noble Truths.'

James listed the Four Noble Truths.

Noble Truth 1: All living things feel unhappiness and suffering.
Noble Truth 2: There is a cause for all unhappiness and suffering.
Noble Truth 3: If you sort out the cause, unhappiness and suffering can be cured.
Noble Truth 4: This is the cure for unhappiness and suffering.

'Suffering is caused by us being selfish and greedy,' James continued. 'We always want things. We want the latest game or trainers. We want an exciting holiday. We want to be healthy and young forever. We think that having these things will make us happy. But none of them can make us truly happy.'

'Why not?' asked Sara, thinking fondly about her new bike.

'Because none of them lasts forever,' replied James. 'This makes us unhappy because we want to cling on to them. The game or latest trainers will break or wear out. The exciting holiday always ends. Everyone gets sick, grows old, and dies sometime.'

James paused and looked around. The others were waiting impatiently for him to tell them about the cure for this unhappiness.

'Our teachers help us to understand three things which cure unhappiness and suffering. They teach us to accept that nothing lasts forever. They teach us to stop being selfish and greedy. They teach us to show love and kindness to all living things. When we understand and do these three things, we will be truly happy.'

Hana suddenly leapt up from where she was sitting.

'These are difficult lessons to learn!' she exclaimed. 'You need very good teachers to help you understand them. We are lucky because in our Buddhist group we have a long line of good teachers. They have passed on the teachings from teacher to disciple for centuries. These teachers always know how to teach people in the best way.'

Hana showed them pictures of some of the great teachers. The line of teachers begins with Buddha Shakyamuni in the sixth century BCE. He lived and taught in India. The teachings were passed on to Atisha who took them to Tibet. In Tibet, Je Tsongkhapa was a very famous teacher. The teachings stayed in Tibet for many centuries until a teacher called Geshe Kelsang Gyatso Rinpoche appeared.

Rees and Sara looked closely at the picture of Geshe Kelsang Gyatso Rinpoche.

'Geshe Kelsang Gyatso Rinpoche decided to move to Britain,' informed Hana. 'He wanted to take the teachings to the rest of the world. He has set up Buddhist centres in this country, Europe, and the United States of America.'

By the end of the afternoon, Rees and Sara knew a little bit more about their friends, James and Hana. Buddhist teachings help James and Hana to learn important things about life. They are taught how they can be truly happy. But the lessons are not easy. James and Hana need to have very good teachers if they are going to understand them properly.

18

4 Caring for the world and others

Rees and Sara struggled into their wellington boots and zipped up their coats. Outside, the sky was overcast and grey. It had been raining. A damp earthy smell was hanging heavily in the air. The leaves had almost finished falling from the trees. It was November.

Rees and Sara walked to the park with their friends, James and Hana. They were taking part in a tree planting project there.

At the park the organiser, Jac, explained why they were planting trees. He said that many trees are vanishing from the planet. Some trees are cut down. Other trees are damaged, or grow old and die. Many of these trees are not replaced by new trees. Jac said that fewer trees may mean all sorts of problems for life on earth.

Trees help to make the air healthy for us to breathe. Trees can affect weather and climate. Trees are homes to many different kinds of wildlife. Trees also look good and this can make us feel better. Without trees the world would be a very different place.

Rees and Sara enjoyed planting trees with James and Hana. They were pleased to be doing something useful to help themselves and other living things.

'We must come back soon and see how our trees are getting on,' said Hana.

'Yes,' agreed James. 'Planting trees is a very Buddhist thing to do. Buddhists believe that everything we do should be helpful to ourselves and others. We should avoid doing anything which harms anyone or anything. Planting trees, like we did today, is helpful. Chopping trees down, and not replacing them, is harmful.'

'That makes sense,' said Sara. 'But why do people want to harm themselves and other living things in the first place? That does not make any sense!'

'Buddhists have an answer for that too!' laughed James. 'Come back to our house. There is a painting in our living room which explains why people do harmful things.'

Rees and Sara gazed up at the painting on the wall.

'The painting is called the Wheel of Life,' explained Hana. 'It tells the story of human beings. People do harmful things to themselves and others. The three animals in the centre of the wheel tell us why. The pig is a symbol for ignorance. The snake is a symbol for hatred. The cockerel is a symbol for greed. All the harmful things people do are caused by ignorance, hatred, and greed.'

Sara thought for a moment before saying, 'Does that mean that people who cut down trees and do not replace them are showing ignorance? They do not really understand the damage they are causing.'

'Yes,' said Hana. 'They are also being greedy. They are thinking about the money they can earn. They are not thinking about others.'

'What do the other parts of the painting mean?' asked Rees.

'The other parts of the painting show what happens when we allow ignorance, hatred and greed to rule our lives. We become trapped in a wheel of pain and suffering,' answered James.

James pointed to the circle on the outside of the picture. 'This shows a human life,' he told them. 'A person is born, lives, and dies and is then reborn into a different body. This happens again and again. You can be reborn into many different kinds of body. In the next circle it shows that you can be reborn as a god, demi-god, human, animal, hungry ghost, or hell creature. What you are reborn as depends on how much ignorance, hatred, and greed you have.'

'There is some good news, though!' continued James. 'We do not have to live in this wheel of pain and suffering forever.'

He pointed to Buddha Shakyamuni who was outside the wheel and said, 'We can be like Buddha. He is truly happy because he has no ignorance, greed, or hatred. He is full of love and kindness for all living things. Buddhists believe that we can be like this too if we follow the Buddhist path.'

Rees and Sara had spent a wonderful afternoon planting trees with their friends James and Hana. They now knew that Buddhists think that it is important to look after the world. Buddhists want to learn how to be loving and kind to all living things. This means leaving behind ignorance, greed, and hatred which makes people unhappy.

24

5 It is better not to kill

Rees and Sara were huddled around a table drinking milkshakes and eating cakes with their friends James and Hana. They were sitting in a very special coffee shop. It was special for two reasons. The first reason was that James and Hana's mother worked there. This meant that the children could visit the coffee shop for treats occasionally. The second reason was that it was an organic coffee shop run by Buddhists.

'Our mother works here because she is a Buddhist,' said James. 'Buddhists believe that we should choose our jobs carefully. We should try to do jobs that do not harm ourselves or other living things. In this coffee shop the food and drinks are organic, which means that they are grown as naturally as possibly. We believe that a lot of food is grown in a way that hurts the world as well as our bodies.'

'This means that our mother knows that she is protecting the environment and other people in her job,' finished Hana.

Rees and Sara started thinking about hundreds of different kinds of jobs. They wondered which jobs Buddhists would be happy doing.

'There is no meat on the menu,' noticed Sara.

'One of our rules is that it is better not to kill,' explained Hana. 'This means that many Buddhists are vegetarians. We believe that harming life, even animal life, is wrong. There is a story about a Tibetan Buddhist monk which shows how important all life is to Buddhists.'

There was an old Tibetan monk who spent a lot of time meditating by a pool of water. Every time the same thing happened. He sat himself down carefully and started meditating. Almost immediately an insect fell into the pool and started thrashing around. Each time the old monk gently reached out and rescued the poor creature. This happened so many times that it was difficult for him to do any serious meditation.

One day, some of the other monks approached him.

'When you meditate you are supposed to be calm and focused,' said one monk. 'How can you be calm and focused if you have to rescue insects all the time? You cannot meditate like that!'

Another monk also spoke to him.

'The pool is not the best place to sit,' he advised. 'You spend all your time saving the lives of insects. You should be meditating. Choose another place to sit!'

The old monk smiled and said, 'When I started on the Buddhist path I made a promise. I promised that I would help every living thing that was in pain and suffering. How can I sit and meditate on love and kindness when these insects need my help?'

'The rule that it is better not to kill is understood by Buddhist groups in different ways,' said James. 'Theravada Buddhist monks are not allowed to till the soil. They are afraid of accidentally killing little creatures living there. So, people give them food every day. Zen Buddhist monks are allowed to till the soil because they need to provide food for themselves. But they would not deliberately kill anything.'

Hana had another idea. 'Whether you kill animals for food or not can depend on how far you have progressed on the Buddhist path,' she said. 'People are at different places on the path. Some people are very skilled and give a lot of time to it. Others are not so skilled and cannot give as much time to it. Everyone does what they can.'

Over milkshakes and cake, Rees and Sara got to know their friends, James and Hana, even better. They now knew that Buddhists try not to kill or harm any living creature deliberately. This means that many Buddhists are vegetarians. But not all Buddhists are the same. Different Buddhist groups understand the rule about not taking life in different ways. Also, some Buddhists are stricter than others because they are further along the Buddhist path.

When Rees and Sara left the coffee shop, they decided that they would share some of their own special things with James and Hana. Maybe they would start next weekend …

In the World Faiths Today Series Rees and Sara learn about the major world faiths in their own country. The seven stories in the series are:

- Exploring Islam
- Exploring Judaism
- Exploring the Parish Church
- Exploring the Orthodox Church
- Exploring Hinduism
- Exploring Buddhism
- Exploring Sikhism

Welsh National Centre for Religious Education
Bangor University
Bangor
Gwynedd
Wales

© Welsh National Centre for Religious Education, 2008.

All rights reserved. These materials are subject to copyright and may not be reproduced or published without the permission of the copyright owner.

First published 2008.

Sponsored by the Welsh Assembly Government.

British Library Cataloguing-in-Publication Data
A catalogue record for this book is available from the British Library.

ISBN 978-1-85357-188-6

Printed and bound in Wales by Gwasg Dwyfor.